EASTER JOKES FOR KIDS

KIDS

BY

Printed Worldwide
First Printing, 2017

ISBN : 1544075219

1. How do you know the Easter Bunny is really intelligent?

Because he's an Egghead!

2. Where does the Easter Bunny get his eggs?

From Eggplants!

3. **What happened to the Easter Bunny when he was bad at school?**

He was eggspelled!

4. **Did you hear about the lady whose house was infested with Easter eggs?**

She had to call an eggs-terminator!

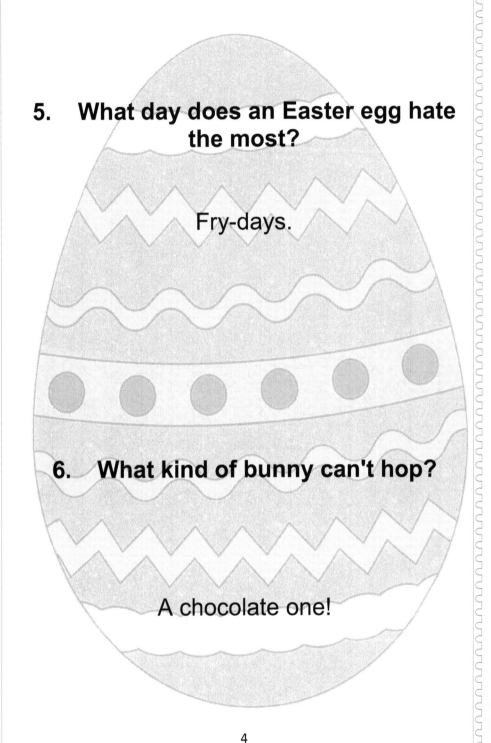

5.   What day does an Easter egg hate the most?

Fry-days.

6.   What kind of bunny can't hop?

A chocolate one!

7. Why did the Easter egg hide?

He was a little chicken!

8. What do you call a rabbit with bed bugs?

Bugs Bunny!

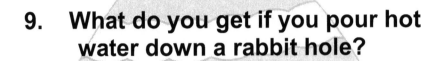

9. **What do you get if you pour hot water down a rabbit hole?**

A hot cross bunny!

10. **How do bunnies stay healthy?**

Eggercise!

11. What do you call a bunny with a dictionary in his pants?

A smarty pants.

12. What do you call Easter when you are hopping around?

Hoppy Easter!

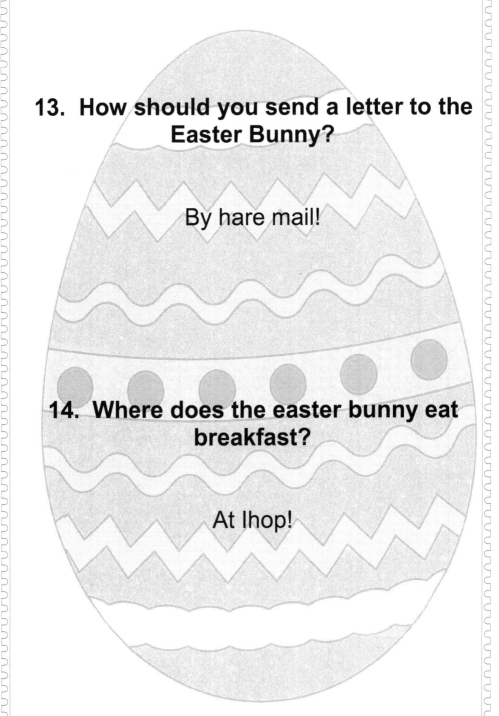

13. How should you send a letter to the Easter Bunny?

By hare mail!

14. Where does the easter bunny eat breakfast?

At Ihop!

15. How long does the Easter Bunny like to party?

Around the cluck!

16. What happened to the easter egg when he was tickled too much?

He cracked up!

17. What do you call a tired Easter egg?

Egg-zosted!

18. Why was the Easter Bunny so annoyed?

He was having a bad hare day!

19. How did the Easter Bunny dry himself with after a shower?

With a hare dryer!

20. "Why are you studying your Easter candy?"

"I'm trying to decide which came first-the chocolate chicken or the chocolate egg!"

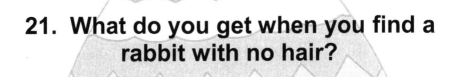

21. What do you get when you find a rabbit with no hair?

A hairless hare!

22. How can you find the Easter bunny?

Eggs (x) marks the spot!

23. Why was the rabbit rubbing his head?

Because he had a eggache!

24. Why was the Easter Bunny at the police station?

He was charged with Hare-assment!

25. **What did the rabbit say to the carrot he was friends with?**

It's been nice gnawing at you!

26. **What has long ears, four legs, and is worn on your head?**

An Easter bunnet!

27. Where does Valentine's Day comes after Easter?

In the dictionary!

28. How do you catch the Easter Bunny?

Hide up a tree and make a noise like a carrot!

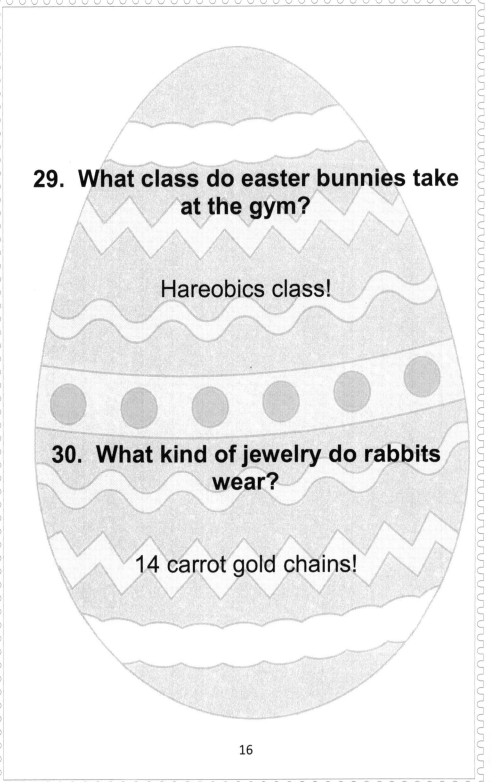

29. What class do easter bunnies take at the gym?

Hareobics class!

30. What kind of jewelry do rabbits wear?

14 carrot gold chains!

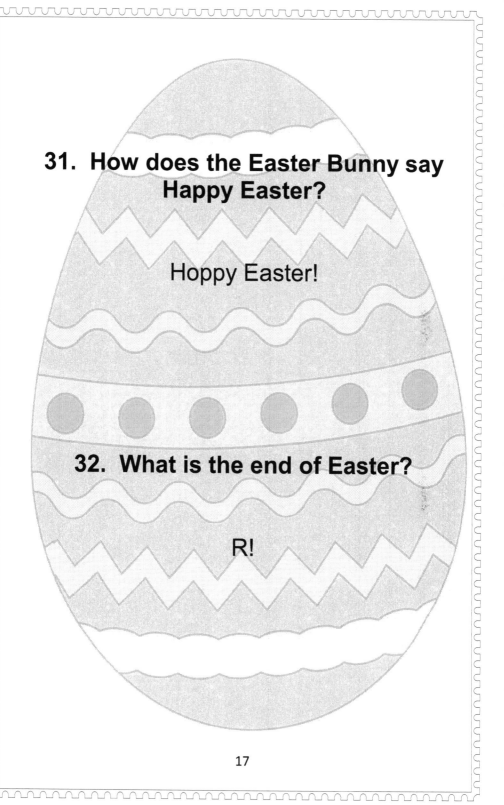

31. How does the Easter Bunny say Happy Easter?

Hoppy Easter!

32. What is the end of Easter?

R!

33. Knock, Knock.

Who's there?

Esther

Esther who?

Esther Bunny

34. What do you call rabbits that marched in a long sweltering Easter parade?

Hot, cross bunnies.

35. What happened when the Easter Bunny met the rabbit of his dreams?

They lived hoppily ever after!

36. What is the Easter Bunny's favourite state capital?

Albunny, New York!

37. **What do you call an egg from outer space?**

An "Egg-stra terrestial".

38. **Where does the Easter Bunny go when he has lost his tail?**

To a re-tail store!

39. Who is the Easter Bunny's favourite movie actor?

Rabbit De Niro!

40. What's yellow, has long ears, and grows on trees?

The Easter Bunana!

41. Why are you stuffing all that Easter candy into your mouth?"

"Because it doesn't taste as good if I stuff it in my ears!"

42. Did you hear the one about the Easter Bunny who sat on a bee?

It's a tender tail!

43. What would you get if you crossed the Easter Bunny with Chinese food?

Hop suey!

44. What did the mommy egg say to the baby egg?

You're "Egg-stra special!"

45. Why did the Easter Bunny cross the road?

Because the chicken had his Easter eggs!

46. How does the Easter Bunny go on holiday?

By hare-plane!

47. How did the Easter Bunny rate the Easter parade?

He said it was eggs-cellent!

48. What do you call a rabbit that tells good jokes?

A funny bunny!

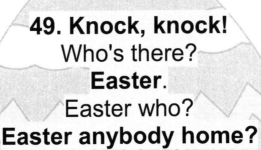

49. Knock, knock!
Who's there?
Easter.
Easter who?
Easter anybody home?

50. **What's the best way to send a letter to the Easter Bunny?**

Hare mail!

51. How does the Easter Bunny keep his fur neat?

With a hare brush!

52. How do you know carrots are good for your eyes?

Have you ever seen a rabbit wearing glasses when he reads?!

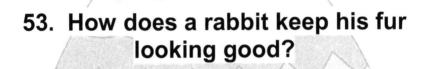

53. How does a rabbit keep his fur looking good?

With hare spray!

54. Why did the bunny go to the dance?

To do the bunny hop!

55. What kinds of books do bunnies like?

Ones with hoppy endings!

56. Why is a bunny the luckiest animal in the world?

Because it has four rabbit's feet!

57. What did the rabbits do after their wedding?

Went on their bunnymoon!

58. Why can't a rabbit's nose be 12 inches long?

Because then it would be a foot!

59. Why did the Easter Bunny cross the road?

To prove he wasn't chicken!

60. What do you get if you cross an elephant with a rabbit?

An elephant who never forgets to eat his carrots!

61. What do you call a dumb bunny?

A hare brain!

62. Why shouldn't you tell an Easter egg a joke?

It might crack up whilst laughing!

63. Why didn't the bunny hop?

No bunny knows.

64. How does the Easter Bunny paint all the Easter eggs?

He hires Santa's elves during the off season.

65. Why do rabbits eat carrots?

Because they don't want to be nearsighted!

66. What kind of music do bunnies like?

Hip Hop!

34

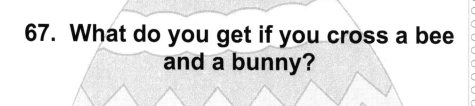

67. What do you get if you cross a bee and a bunny?

A honey bunny!

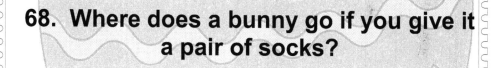

68. Where does a bunny go if you give it a pair of socks?

A sock hop!

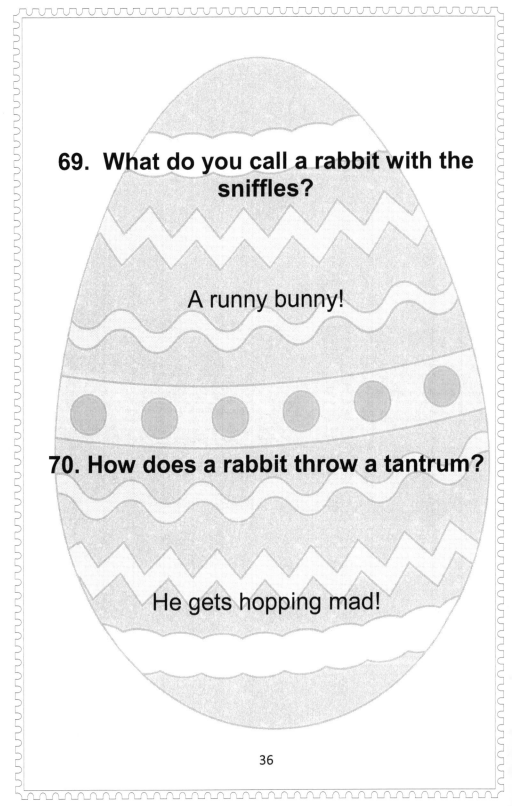

69. What do you call a rabbit with the sniffles?

A runny bunny!

70. How does a rabbit throw a tantrum?

He gets hopping mad!

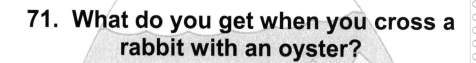

71. What do you get when you cross a rabbit with an oyster?

The oyster bunny.

72. What kind of beans grow in the Easter Bunny's garden?

Jelly beans!

73. What did the Easter Egg say to the other Easter Egg?

Have you heard any good yolks today?

74. Knock Knock

Who's there?

Some bunny

Some bunny who?

Some bunny has been eating my Easter candy!

75. How can you tell how old a rabbit is?

Just look for the gray hares!

76. What is a dog's favorite Easter treat?

Jelly bones!

77. What do you need if your chocolate eggs mysteriously disappear?

You need an eggsplanation!

78. How is the Easter Bunny like Michael Jordan?

They're both famous for stuffing baskets!

79. What's red and blue and sogs up your Easter basket?

Coloured scrambled eggs!

80. Did you hear about the farmer who fed crayons to his chickens?

He wanted them to lay coloured eggs!

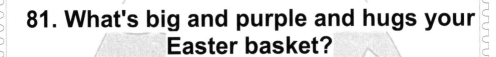

81. What's big and purple and hugs your Easter basket?

The Easter Barney!

82. Who delivers Easter treats to all the fish in the sea?

The Oyster Bunny!

83. What did the carrot say to the rabbit?

Do you want to grab a bite?

84. How do Easter chicks leave a building?

By the emergency egg-sit!

85. Why do we paint Easter eggs?

Because it's too hard to wallpaper them!

86. What do you call someone who is addicted to eggs?

An egg-oholic

87. How does a rabbit make gold soup?

He begins with 24 carrots.

88. What did one easter bunny sing to the other?

"I'm so egg-cited I just can't hide it!"

89. What did my teacher say to me before the easter holidays?

Have an egg-celent easter!

90. What did one easter egg say to the other easter egg about his DIY?

You best get cracking!

91. How did the egg climb the mountain?

It scrambled up!

92. How do comedians like their eggs?

Funny side up!

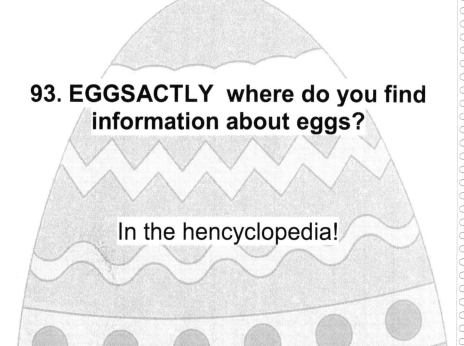

93. EGGSACTLY where do you find information about eggs?

In the hencyclopedia!

94. Why is the Easter bunny so popular?

Because he is egg-stra special!

95. Did you hear about the story about the rainbow Colored Easter egg?

Well I have been dying to tell you!

96. What did one easter egg say to his shy friend?

To show your true colors, you have to come out of your shell!

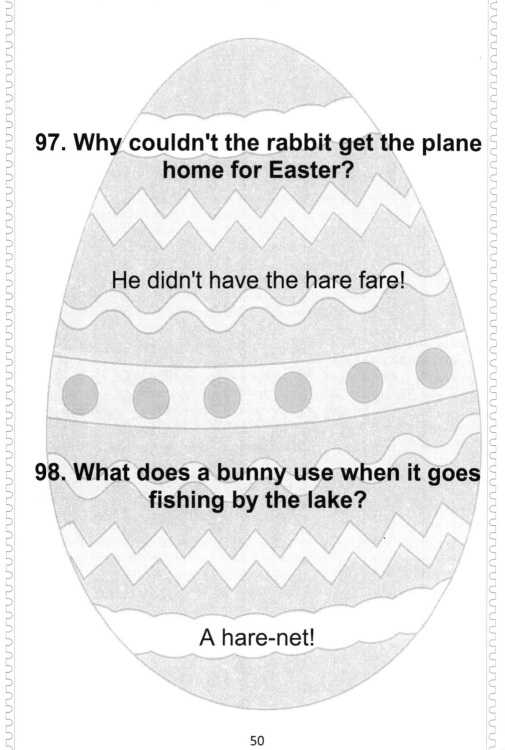

97. Why couldn't the rabbit get the plane home for Easter?

He didn't have the hare fare!

98. What does a bunny use when it goes fishing by the lake?

A hare-net!

99. Why are people always tired in April?

Because they've just finished a 31 day March!

100. What do you call ten rabbits marching backwards?

A receding hareline.

101. Why does Peter Cottontail hop down the bunny trail?

Because he is too young to drive!

102. How do you know the Easter Bunny liked his trip?

Because he said it was egg-cellent!

103. Knock, Knock?
Who's there?

Ana

Ana who?

Ana-other Easter Bunny!

104. What stories does the Easter Bunny like best?

The ones with happy eggings!

105. Why didn't the bunny hop?

No bunny knows.

106. What does a bunny rabbit do in the rain?

Get wet!

107. Once there were two chocolate bunnies and one had their ear bit off. One said, "Happy Easter."

The other one said, "what?!"

108. How do you make a rabbit stew?

Make it wait for ten hours!

109. What did the gray rabbit say to the blue rabbit?

Cheer up!

110. What do you call the Easter Bunny the Monday after Easter?

Tired.

111. How many chocolate bunnies can you put into an empty Easter basket?

Only one because after that, it's not empty!

112. What do Easter Bunny helpers get for making a basket?

Two points, just like anyone else who plays basketball!

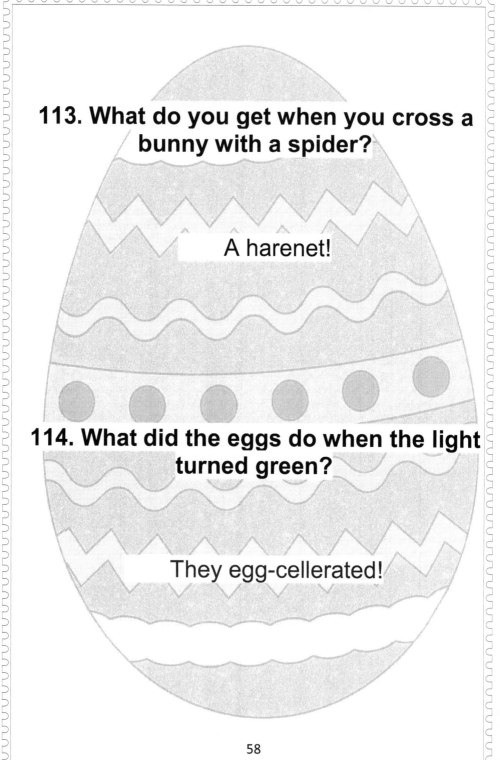

113. What do you get when you cross a bunny with a spider?

A harenet!

114. What did the eggs do when the light turned green?

They egg-cellerated!

115. How do easter bunnies leave a room?

Through the egg-sit!

116. Why did the easter bunny go to school?

To get an egg-ucation!

117. What's the best way to catch a unique rabbit?

Unique up on him.

118. How do you catch a tame rabbit?

Tame way, unique up on it!

119. How many hairs in a rabbit's tail?

None, they're all on the outside.

120. How do you know when you're eating rabbit stew?

When it has hares in it!

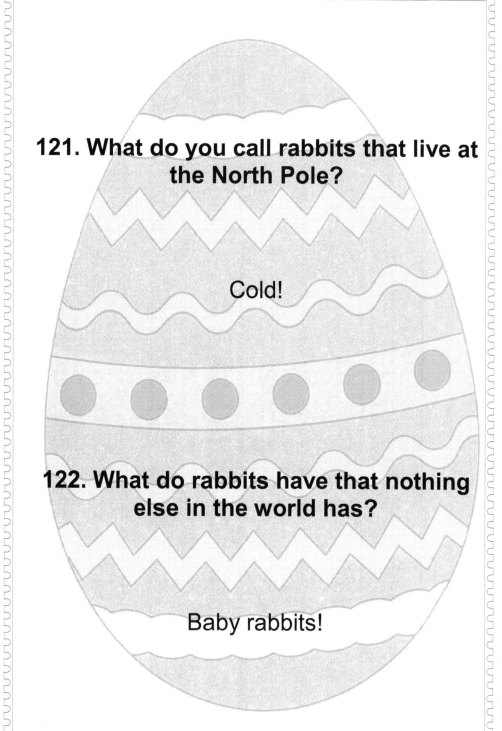

121. What do you call rabbits that live at the North Pole?

Cold!

122. What do rabbits have that nothing else in the world has?

Baby rabbits!

123. Waitress, what's this hare doing in my soup?

Looks like the back stroke!

124. What do you call an easter bunny with a dictionary in his trousers?

A smarty pants!

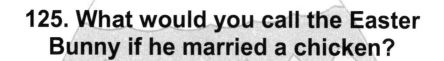

125. What would you call the Easter Bunny if he married a chicken?

The first Rabbit to lay and egg!

126. What did the bunny say when he only had thistles to eat?

Thistle have to do!

127. What's the difference between a fake dollar bill and a crazy rabbit?

One is bad money, the other is a mad bunny!

128. How did the Easter Bunny rate the Easter parade?

He said it was eggs-cellent!

129. Where does Dracula keep his Easter candy?

In his Easter casket!

130. A man wanted an Easter pet for his daughter. He looked at a baby chick and a baby duck. They were both cute, but he decided to buy the baby chick. Do you know why?

The baby chick was a little cheaper!

131. What do you call an Easter bunny from outer space?

An egg-straterrestrial.

132. Why did the Easter Bunny have to fire the duck?

He kept quacking the eggs!

133. What did the easter bunny say about his chocolate?

It was egg-celent!

134. Man: What's the difference between the Easter rabbit and a mattababy?

Lady: What's a mattababy?

Man: Nothing. What's the matter with you?

135. What do you call a chocolate bunny that was out in the sun too long?

A runny bunny!

136. What do you get when you cross a rabbit with a boyscout?

A boyscout who helps little old ladies hop across the street.

137. What do you call an easter egg in the caribbean?

Melted!

138. What do you get when you cross the easter bunny with an onion?

An easter bunion!

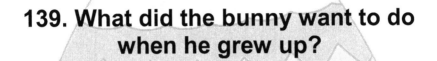

139. What did the bunny want to do when he grew up?

Join the Hare Force in the army!

140. What goes ha-ha-clunk?

A bunny laughing its butt off!

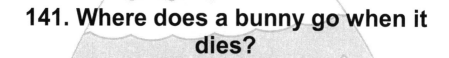

141. Where does a bunny go when it dies?

To the hare-after!

142. What's the difference between a bunny and a lumberjack?

One chews and hops, the other hews and chops!

143. Why did the magician have to cancel his show?

He'd just washed his hare and couldn't do a thing with it!

144. Why does the easter bunny have such a shiny nose?

His powder puff's on the wrong end!

145. What do you call it when a rabbit has an accident with a knife?

A hare cut!

146. What came first, the chicken or the egg?

Neither--the Easter Bunny did!

147. Knock, knock.

Who's there?

Dewey

Dewey who?

Dewey have to listen to any more easter bunny jokes!

148. What is the Easter Bunny's favorite sport?

Basket-ball, of course!

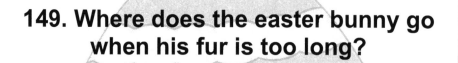

149. Where does the easter bunny go when his fur is too long?

To the haredressers!

150. What kind of easter bunny is never on time?

A ChocoLATE one!

79

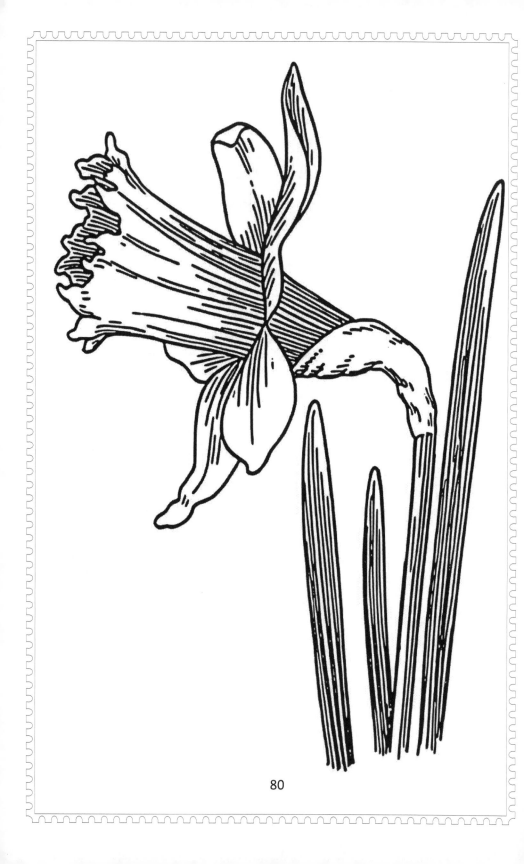

Easter Word Search

```
G  Q  S  B  N  M  G  P  N  L  P  L  S  R  M  O  G  N  H  S
C  Q  M  Z  A  W  Q  J  I  O  Z  M  I  V  B  S  L  U  F  X
A  A  V  L  M  L  D  D  X  R  J  L  Z  D  C  N  P  C  O  L
L  T  Y  T  H  Y  F  D  Z  Y  O  U  E  L  O  V  Z  W  H  K
A  K  S  P  R  I  N  G  I  S  Y  U  T  R  X  F  H  G  Z  V
S  S  T  M  B  A  S  R  D  B  R  Q  S  M  G  U  F  D  H  U
A  O  F  B  Z  U  N  T  A  T  H  K  R  O  G  R  Q  A  J  J
J  D  W  K  V  N  N  B  O  N  E  G  Z  Z  E  K  G  T  D  L
E  V  Y  M  U  M  G  N  O  T  C  R  F  H  I  W  R  S  G  V
T  O  Q  R  C  F  E  H  Y  L  I  E  G  W  L  Z  H  G  Y  U
A  A  K  B  P  E  S  U  M  B  H  Q  E  U  W  Z  J  N  Q  M
L  S  V  T  E  A  Z  A  L  Z  C  I  S  Y  D  S  I  E  I  N
O  W  C  Z  Y  T  D  S  P  D  C  D  T  O  V  P  H  A  P  H
C  A  A  H  I  S  F  M  L  O  Q  U  B  N  W  B  L  P  E  E
O  F  H  G  J  B  V  F  Q  C  F  G  K  F  H  R  O  A  X  A
H  M  L  R  G  N  E  D  O  P  S  T  U  Y  A  A  H  C  V  N
C  T  Y  S  Z  J  Y  H  B  N  H  Y  O  T  K  F  A  X  J  D
L  Z  W  E  T  U  B  U  T  T  E  R  F  L  Y  F  U  C  H  Q
P  A  P  I  A  Y  R  A  B  B  I  T  G  H  Z  T  P  Y  H  I
I  N  J  F  W  M  R  W  I  W  P  D  B  K  G  J  A  W  J  P
```

BABY	BUTTERFLY	RABBIT	EGG
DAFFODIL	LAMB	CHOCOLATE	CHIC
BUNNY	SPRING		

Help the Easter bunny find his eggs

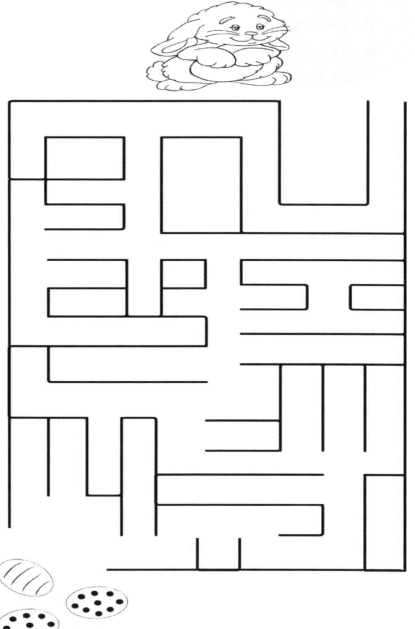

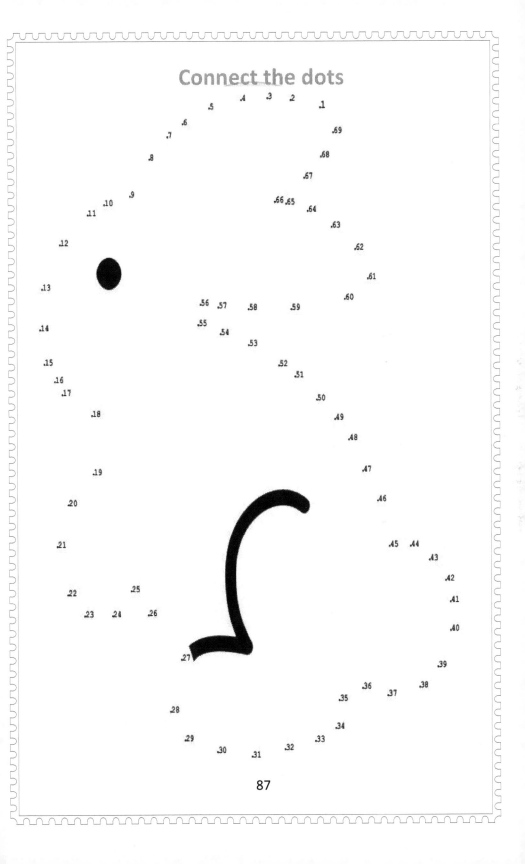

Easter Word Scramble

Please unscramble the words below

1. atrsEe

_____

2. bynnu

_____

3. abirbt

_____

4. lofwre

_____

5. hcloactoe

_____

Made in the USA
San Bernardino, CA
11 April 2017